Canadian
Endangered Species

By Colleayn O. Mastin 🐾 *Illustrated by Jan Sovak*

Grasshopper
BOOKS PUBLISHING

A portion of the sales of this book will be donated to the Canadian Nature Federation

Black Footed Ferret

Near the burrows of the prairie dog
The black-footed ferret once thrived;
Where prairie dogs set up a "town",
The black-footed ferret arrived.

But prairie dog's homes grew fewer,
When their grasslands were taken away;
Then the black footed ferret discovered
That it had no place to stay.

Before people came to the prairies, there were thousands of small, brown, burrowing prairie dogs, the favorite food of the black footed ferret. When the prairie dogs seemed to be eating too much of the farmer's grass, they were killed by poisoning and hunting.

This led to the disappearance of the ferret. For as well as eating prairie dogs, these ferrets would often take over their burrows, and make their homes in the middle of a prairie dog town.

Before ferrets became a seriously endangered species, the female would give birth to three to five young ones in late spring.

Today, the black-footed ferret is described as "the rarest North American mammal".

Cougar

The mountain lion or cougar,
Is a sly and stealthy cat,
It truly is carnivorous,
Eats moose and things like that.

This solitary hunter
Is very hard to see,
As it creeps through mountain forests,
As hungry as can be.

The cougar is the largest cat in Canada. This fierce cat is endangered in the eastern parts of Canada, but seems to be surviving quite well in the mountains of Alberta and British Columbia.

Cougar skin and meat have little value, but a cougar pelt is often used as a trophy-rug or wall-hanging. Hunting, trapping, poisonings, and the taking over of its habitat by people, are reasons that it is endangered. Other than humans, the cougar's only enemy is the wolf.

Cougars prefer to eat deer, but beaver, rabbits, birds, and even mice and frogs are also hunted for food. They sometimes attack cattle.

In midsummer, female cougars give birth to two or three kittens. They are raised only by the mother, and they stay with her for a year.

This small, brown, marmot likes to live
On a rocky mountain side;
It burrows in among the rocks,
Where it can sleep or hide.

It keeps busy in the summer months,
Eating flowers and fruit all day;
But when September rolls around,
It goes to bed till May!

After nine months of hibernation, marmots mate. Then, about one month later, four or five young marmots join the small colony that lives together in a large burrow dug in the ground. Marmots never wander far from their home burrow.

They are playful animals, and two marmots often engage in what seems to be a wrestling match, standing on their hindlegs and pushing at each other. Their favorite food is plants, berries, and flowers.

The only place in the world that this marmot is found is on some high mountains on Vancouver Island. One reason they are endangered is because logging developments and ski resorts are gradually taking over their habitat. Today, there are fewer than three hundred of this species alive.

Whooping Crane

The tallest bird in Canada
Is called the whooping crane;
Where once it had its breeding grounds,
There now are fields of grain.

These beautiful great fliers
Have wings two meters wide;
They soar aloft on rising air,
Then elegantly glide.

Each winter, whooping cranes make a long and dangerous flight from north Canada to Texas. Then, in April they return to their northern nesting grounds. Here the female lays two eggs in a large nest made of bulrushes. Usually, only one of the two chicks that hatch survives.

To increase the survival rate of the chicks, naturalists have used sandhill cranes as "foster parents". They remove an egg from a whooping crane's nest and place it in a sandhill crane's nest, where it will have a better chance to hatch out as healthy chick.

At one time, there were only fifteen whooping cranes alive. Now there are more than two hundred. It is against the law to harm a whooping crane.

11

The falcon is the Prince of Birds,
A creature of great power;
When diving downward, it can reach
Three hundred "k's" per hour.

This bird of prey has strong, clawed feet,
Hooked beak, and super eyes;
When it attacks a bird in flight,
The end is no surprise.

Peregrine Falcon

Despite its great power, the peregrine falcon is in danger of becoming extinct. People who like to tame falcons in order to hunt with them, have robbed or disturbed their nesting sites.

Another reason for this falcon's decline, is pesticide poisoning. The falcons themselves may not die of the poison, but the pesticides cause problems with the development of the two to four eggs that are produced each year. The eggs are often brittle, break easily, or do not hatch at all.

Female falcons are considerably bigger than male falcons. The eggs laid by the female are looked after by both parents.

Spotted Owl

To see a spotted owl
Is a sight that's very rare;
In the mountains of the west coast,
They are down to a few pair.

They live in old growth forests
Fly at night, but not by day,
When human beings disturb them,
These owls move away.

Normally, spotted owls stay close to home all the year round. But when the old growth forests where they live are threatened by roads and logging, they have to find a safer place to build new nests.

Spotted owls hunt only at night, feeding on squirrels and other small rodents. They have very large black eyes which allow them to see in the dark. When they hoot, it sounds something like the barking of a dog.

In a nest high up in a tall coniferous tree, the females of this rare species lay two or three plain white eggs. These owls are still in danger of extinction. The spotted owl population in Canada is probably no more than fifteen pairs.

A beluga whale is noisy,
It can sing and whistle and scream;
Its shortish body is round and plump,
With skin the color of cream.

This whale is not a great diver,
It likes shallow waters instead;
When it wants to get a breath of air,
It breaks through the ice with its head.

There were once thousands of beluga whales in the St. Lawrence River, but now there are fewer than seven hundred. Although this whale is protected, chemical pollution in the river threatens its ability to survive and increase its numbers.

It is also thought that the noise made by the busy St. Lawrence traffic makes it difficult for the whales to communicate with one another.

St. Lawrence River

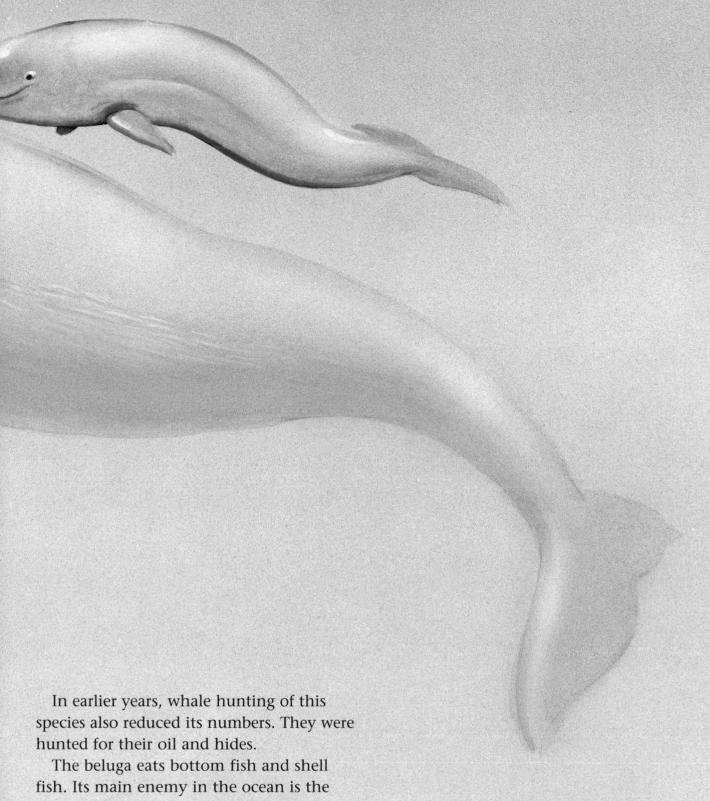

In earlier years, whale hunting of this species also reduced its numbers. They were hunted for their oil and hides.

The beluga eats bottom fish and shell fish. Its main enemy in the ocean is the killer whale.

Beluga Whale

Bowhead Whale

A bowhead is a "baleen" whale
That means it feeds on "krill",
Those millions of tiny plankton
This whale needs to get its fill.

A bowhead whale is large and slow,
With a great big head and mouth.
In spring, it migrates to the north;
In fall,it swims back south.

Bowhead whales like to live close to ice-flows in the Canadian Arctic waters.

Because bowhead whales are slow-moving and have a valuable store of blubber, whaling ships have hunted them since the 1840's. Only a few, still swim in the cold northern waters. The only people who are permitted to hunt bowhead whales are the Inuit people in the north. Their only enemies are man and the killer whale.

Right Whale

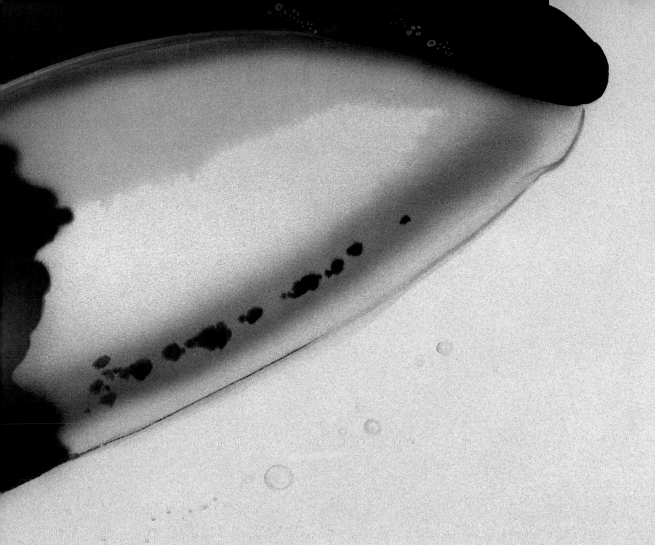

This whale was easy to capture
Because it was big and slow;
So whalers thought it the "right" whale
To hunt, many years ago.

Two other features made it the one
For whalers to chase in their boats:
Its blubber is rich in whale oil,
And when killed, doesn't sink, but floats.

Most whales sink after they have been killed, but since right whales don't, this made them easy for whalers to capture. These right whales produced large quantities of oil that was burned in lamps and used to make soap.

As well as being caught by whalers, right whales have been killed when hit by a ship or accidental capture in fishing nets. In 1946 right whales were declared a protected species. There are now about four thousand swimming in the oceans of the world.

A female gives birth to one calf every three to four years. The young calf is nearly five meters long at birth.

Leather Back Turtle

Leatherback turtles live in the sea,
But nest on the warm, sandy shore,
Where the female lays great numbers of eggs,
There are hundreds, maybe more.

This is the world's largest turtle,
It can weigh as much as a car;
It travels wherever it wants to,
In the oceans near and far.

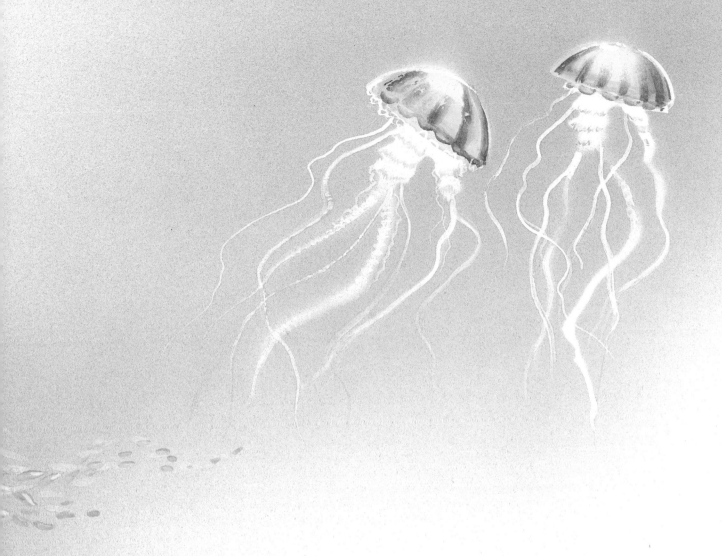

Unlike other large turtles, the leatherback does not have a valuable shell. Nor is it hunted for food, since its meat is not thought tasty enough to eat.

Many creatures, including humans, hunt for and eat the eggs found in sandy nests on the beach. Because of this, not many of the hundreds of eggs that the female lays are hatched successfully. This, plus the killing of turtles for trophy, is a reason for their drastic decline.

Leatherback turtles eat fish, sea urchins, seaweed, and jelly fish. Plastic bags, which can resemble a jelly fish, are sometimes eaten by the unsuspecting turtle. This is another possible reason for their being endangered.

Blanchard's Cricket Frog

This frog is called a "cricket"
Because of its cricket-like song;
When frightened by an enemy,
The leap it takes is long.

This rare and very threatened frog,
Is found at Point Pelee,
In the province of Ontario,
In a park on Lake Erie.

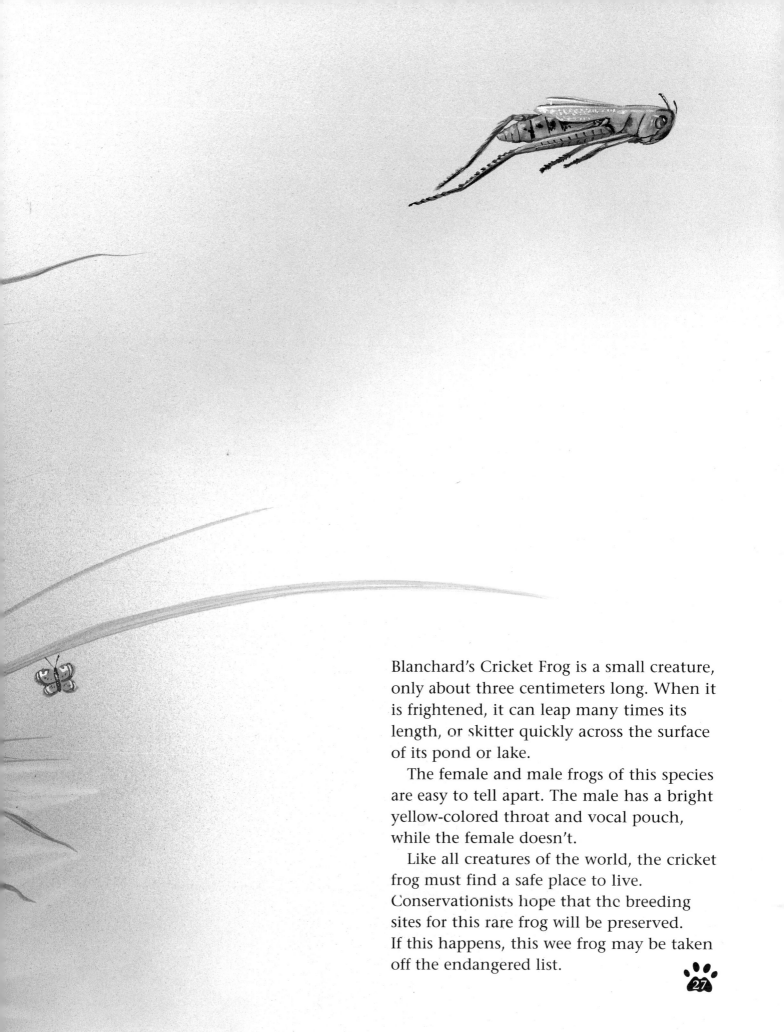

Blanchard's Cricket Frog is a small creature, only about three centimeters long. When it is frightened, it can leap many times its length, or skitter quickly across the surface of its pond or lake.

The female and male frogs of this species are easy to tell apart. The male has a bright yellow-colored throat and vocal pouch, while the female doesn't.

Like all creatures of the world, the cricket frog must find a safe place to live. Conservationists hope that the breeding sites for this rare frog will be preserved. If this happens, this wee frog may be taken off the endangered list.

Spotted Bat

Not much is known about these bats,
Small things with massive ears;
Their spots are three—two on their backs
And one upon their rears.

By day they roost on rocky cliffs,
At night they fly about;
If moths are in their neighborhood,
They'd be wise to fly right out.

Scientists fear that the spotted bat is threatened both by the use of pesticides which poison the bats, and by changing open country into towns.

Bats have very weak eyesight. They navigate in the dark by sending out shrill bat calls that bounce back to their large ears, in the same way that humans use radar.

Bats are the only mammals that can fly. They spend the night flying about catching insects. The spotted bat's favorite food is a moth.

Most bats live in large colonies, but the spotted bat lives by itself. There is a small population of spotted bats in Canada. Most of them live in the dry interior valleys of British Columbia.

Piping Plover

The piping plover builds its nest
On the shore of a lake or ocean;
If anything should threaten it,
This plover will cause a commotion.

Many things threaten the plover,
For their eggs are easy to spot;
If a hungry skunk should find them,
It will gobble up the lot.

When anything approaches a piping plover's nest containing its four spotted eggs, the plover puts on an interesting show. It may fly from its nest and flop down on the sand, pretending to be injured. It does this to draw attention away from its precious eggs.

One reason the plover is endangered is the place where it builds its nest. This is always just above the high-water mark on a lake or ocean. If there is a storm or an especially high tide, the plover's nest and eggs will be washed away.

Another reason for it being endangered is because people build their homes and cottages too close to their nesting areas.

There may be only about two thousands of these birds alive.

Canadian Endangered Species
Text copyright © 1995 by Colleayn O. Mastin
Illustration copyright © 1995 Jan Sovak

Published by
Grasshopper Books Publishing
106 - Waddington Drive
Kamloops, British Columbia
Canada V2E 1M2

This book is dedicated to my three brothers, Jack, Ray & Bud Stout.

Acknowledgments
The author wishes to thank the following:
Committee on the status of Endangered Wildlife in Canada, Wendy Nankievell, Dennis Johnson and my Family.

Designed by Kunz + Associates.
Printed in Canada by Friesen Printers Ltd. Altona, Manitoba.

Canadian Cataloguing in Publication Data
Mastin, Colleayn, O. (Colleayn Olive)
Canadian endangered species
(Nature Canada Series; 5)
ISBN 1-895910 - 08 - 0 (bound)
- ISBN 1 - 895910 - 09 - 9 (pbk.)
1. Endangerd Species –Canada –Juvenile literature.
I. Sovak, Jan, 1953- II. Title. III. Series.
(Colleayn Olive), Nature Canada series ; 5)
QL84.24.M38 1995   j.591.52'9'0971   C94-910360-8